Wood Frogs

by Joyce Markovics

Consultant: Jon P. Costanzo, PhD
Senior Research Scholar and Adjunct Professor of Zoology
Department of Zoology, Miami University
Oxford, Ohio

BEARPORT PUBLISHING

New York, New York

Credits

Cover, © Mark Mirror/Shutterstock; TOC, © Don Mammoser/Shutterstock; 4–5, © Michelle Gilders/Alamy; 6–7, © Dan Minicucci/National Geographic Society; 8–9, © Cary Anderson; 10–11, © Kitchin & Hurst/LeesonPhoto; 12–13, © JM Storey, Carleton University; 14–15, © Ted Kinsman; 16–17, © Sheldon, Allen Blake/Animals Animals/Earth Scenes; 18–19, © Andrew McLachlan/All Canada Photos/Corbis; 19, © Leszczynski, Zigmund/Animals Animals/Earth Scenes; 20–21, © Mark Mirror/Shutterstock; 22T, © Gerald A. DeBoer/Shutterstock; 22B, © Chamelion Studio/Shutterstock; 23TL, © Matt Jeppson/Shutterstock; 23TM, © JM Storey, Carleton University; 23TR, © Jared Hobbs/All Canada Photos/Corbis; 23BL, © Francis Bossé/Shutterstock; 23BR, © Leszczynski, Zigmund/Animals Animals/Earth Scenes.

Publisher: Kenn Goin
Senior Editor: Joyce Tavolacci
Creative Director: Spencer Brinker
Design: Debrah Kaiser
Photo Researcher: Michael Win

Library of Congress Cataloging-in-Publication Data

Markovics, Joyce L., author.
  Wood frogs / by Joyce Markovics ; consultant: Jon P. Costanzo, PhD.
      pages cm. — (In winter, where do they go?)
  Includes bibliographical references and index.
  ISBN 978-1-62724-319-3 (library binding) — ISBN 1-62724-319-4 (library binding)
  1. Wood frog—Juvenile literature. 2. Wood frog—Hibernation—Juvenile literature. I. Title.
  QL668.E27M33 2015
  597.8'9—dc23
                                2014004651

For more information, write to Bearport Publishing Company, Inc., 45 West 21st Street, Suite 3B, New York, New York 10010. Printed in the United States of America.

10 9 8 7 6 5 4 3 2 1

Contents

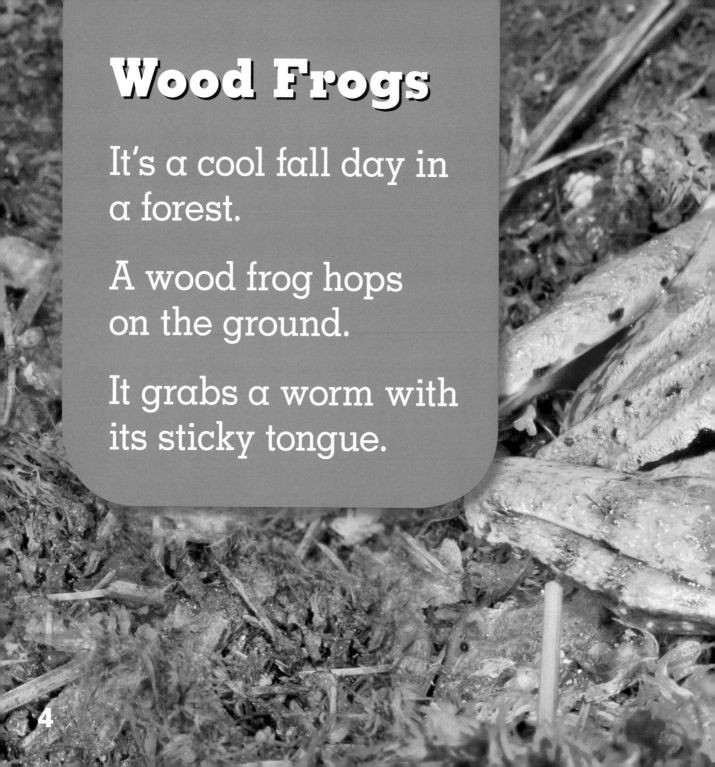

Wood Frogs

It's a cool fall day in a forest.

A wood frog hops on the ground.

It grabs a worm with its sticky tongue.

worm

Wood frogs eat worms, beetles, and flies.

Winter is coming.

Soon, there will be less food to catch.

It will get very cold.

How will the frog **survive**?

Like all frogs, wood frogs are **amphibians**. This group of animals lives in water and on land.

The little frog pushes away some soil and leaves.

It rests and doesn't move.

The frog is **hibernating**.

Wood frogs hibernate on land during winter. Other kinds of frogs hibernate in ponds.

During winter, snow falls.

Then something amazing happens.

When ice touches the frog, its body freezes!

Wood frogs have tan or brown skin.

Water inside the frog's body turns to ice.

The frog's body becomes hard as a rock.

For days or even weeks, the frog stays frozen.

When the frog's body freezes, its heart stops beating.

14

While it is frozen, the frog doesn't eat.

It also doesn't breathe.

The frog's skin blends in with dead leaves. This helps the frog hide from enemies.

15

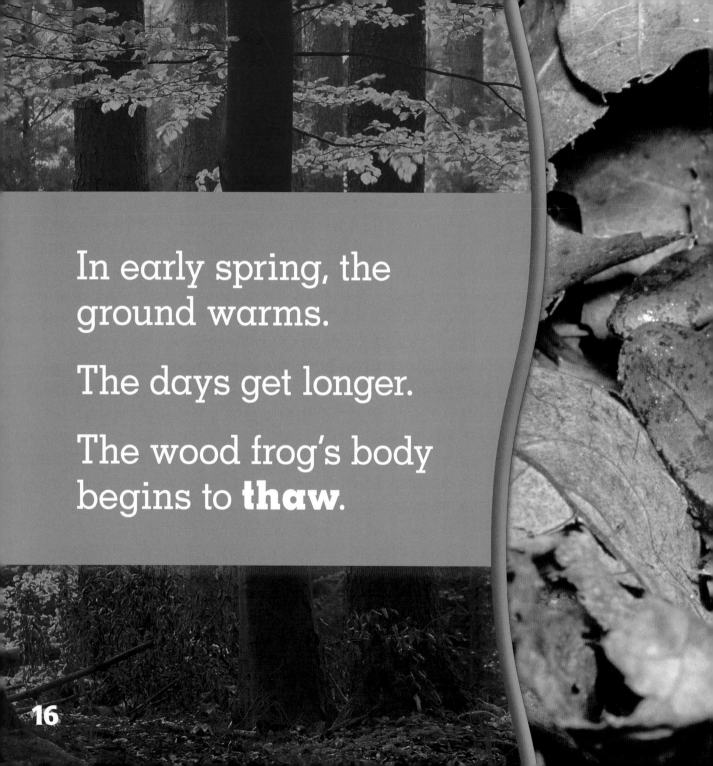

In early spring, the ground warms.

The days get longer.

The wood frog's body begins to **thaw**.

It can take around ten hours for the frog to thaw.

After the frog has thawed, it hops away!

It goes to a pond to **mate**.

There, female wood frogs lay their eggs.

Tadpoles hatch from eggs. After about two months, the tadpoles become small frogs.

After mating, the wood frog returns to the forest.

It will catch lots of bugs in the warm sun.

In a few months, it will be winter.

The frog will freeze once again!

Wood frogs have a dark brown band behind each eye. The band looks like a mask.

21

Wood Frog Facts

There are nearly 6,000 different kinds of frogs. Wood frogs live in North America.

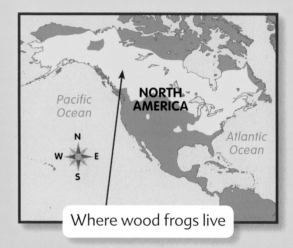

Where wood frogs live

Food: Worms, beetles, flies, and other small animals

Size: 1.4 to 3 inches (3.6 to 7.6 cm) long

Weight: 0.2 to 0.6 ounces (5.7 to 17 g)—or the weight of one or two pencils

Life Span: Up to four years

Cool Fact: Male wood frogs make a quacking sound to attract females.

Size of an adult wood frog

A teacup

Glossary

amphibians
(am-FIB-ee-uhnz)
a group of animals
that live part of their
lives in water and
part on land

hibernating
(HYE-bur-*nayt*-ing)
spending the winter
in a cold, inactive
state

mate (MAYT)
to come together
with another animal
to have young

survive (sur-VIVE)
to stay alive

tadpoles (TAD-pohlz)
young frogs that live
in water before they
become adults

thaw (THAW)
to warm up
and soften

Index

Read More

Bishop, Nic. *Frogs.* New York: Scholastic (2008).

Himmelman, John. *A Wood Frog's Life.* New York: Children's Press (1998).

Learn More Online

To learn more about wood frogs, visit
www.bearportpublishing.com/InWinterWhereDoTheyGo?

About the Author

Joyce Markovics lives along the Hudson River in Tarrytown, New York. She has an aged pet frog who likes to stare out the glass from inside his aquarium.